Me, A Gourmet Cook?

Written by
Carolyn Coats

Illustrations by
Sheila Behr

Thomas Nelson Publishers
Nashville

Dear friends,

As more and more Americans are becoming aware of good nutrition, I have added a new section that will help you to make healthy choices to lighten your diet.

There are three pages of super substitutes and healthy hints that will help you convert favorite recipes, beginning on page 117.

You don't have to be a gourmet cook to have a party! With these simple menus, easy but delicious recipes, you can cook with confidence and entertain with enthusiasm!

Success!
Carolyn Coats

Index to <u>Fun</u> and <u>Easy</u> Entertaining

3

Menu for Dinner for Best Friends

Black Bean Dip
Peanuts on a Pedestal - Low salt, dry roasted
Easy Barbeque Chicken with Noodles
Lettuce Wedges with Bleu Cheese Dressing
Bread - Your favorite
Homemade Peach Cobbler

Real friends are those who, when you've made a fool of yourself, don't think you've done a permanent job.

4

Dinner for Best Friends

5

Black Bean Dip - Quick, delicious, even good for you!

1 can black bean soup
1 8 oz. package light cream cheese
½ of small onion - dash Tabasco to taste
Mix in food processor, blender or mixer. Chop other half of onion and add Tabasco and onion by hand.
This is nice served in a crockery bowl with low-salt corn chips.

Some people think the basic food groups are canned, frozen and take-out.

Try to limit appetizers to
light foods that will not ruin a good appetite. 7.

Your Own Creamy Bleu Cheese Dressing

Combine 1 cup (8 oz. package) crumbled Bleu cheese with 2 cups mayonaise, 1/4 cup vinegar, 2 Tbs. sugar, 1/2 cup sour cream and 1 clove garlic, minced. Beat till fluffy.

Cut lettuce into wedges. One large head of iceberg makes 8 wedges.

You can use Bleu cheese or French dressing in a bottle but add 1 4 oz. package crumbled Bleu cheese and they'll think you're a gourmet.

8

Easy Barbeque Chicken with Noodles

½ stick of margarine

1 package onion soup mix

1 cup hickory flavored barbeque sauce

1 chicken breast for each person or your favorite
   chicken pieces.

While oven is preheating, melt your margarine,
in flat casserole dish. Stir in soup mix and barbeque sauce with margarine, when melted. Add
chicken and turn to coat both sides. Bake at
350° uncovered for one hour. This makes a
marvelous sauce to go over your noodles.

9

Southern Peach Cobbler

One large can sliced Freestone peaches
   or 4 cups fresh peaches, sweetened to taste.
One cup sugar
One stick butter
3/4 cup self-rising flour
3/4 cup milk

   Melt butter in a medium flat casserole dish, 8 X 12, while oven is preheating to 350°. Mix together sugar, flour, milk and pour into melted butter in baking dish. Arrange drained peaches over mixture and bake 1 hour at 350°. Serves 8.

How to make perfect <u>Iced tea</u>

To make 4 glasses of iced tea, measure 2 Tbs. tea or 6 tea bags into teapot. Pour 2 cups fresh, vigorously boiling water over the leaves. Cover and let stand 5 minutes. Stir. Then pour brew through a tea strainer, if you did not use tea bags, into a pitcher. Immediately add 2 cups cold water and let tea cool at room temperature till serving time. Pour tea into tall iced-filled glasses. Offer juicy lemon wedges, sugar or sugar substitutes.

Menu

Pizza Dip
Antipasto
Easy bake Lasagna
Garlic Bread or Breadsticks from the Deli
Tutti - Frutti Tortoni

Things may come to those who wait,
But only the things left by those
who hustle.

An Italian Supper

13

Pizza Dip - No cooking - must be made ahead - Hurrah!

8 oz. cream cheese
1 15½ oz jar Pizza sauce
1 cup chopped green pepper
1 cup chopped onion
1 small can pitted black olives
1 small can of mushrooms, sliced and drained
½ lb. browned ground beef
8 oz. grated Mozzarella cheese

Have a spreader handy. They're going to want lots of this on their chips.

olives

Spread softened cream cheese on a large, flat serving dish. Spread on pizza sauce, peppers and onions. Cover overnight in fridge. Add ground beef, spread cheese over this. Slice olives lengthwise and decorate, too. *P.S. This has a fantastic look & taste!*

Put a candle in a Chianti bottle, make or buy a red checked table cloth, put on some Italian music, prepare these simple recipes, and you'll make Pavarotti want to come to your party!

Antipasto - the classic Italian first course.
A head of lettuce chopped and scattered over a large platter. Dump the following ingredients over lettuce.

4 small tomatoes quartered
1 small jar Cento-Capri pepper salad
⅛ lb. thinly sliced pepperoni
⅛ lb. Provolone cheese crumbled
⅛ lb. Italian dry salami
1 small can pitted, drained black olives.
1 small Bermuda onion sliced very thin.

Drizzle Italian dressing lightly over the whole platter.

Easy Lasagna Bake

One 8 oz. package lasagne noodles, cooked
1 lb. ground beef- I always use ground round.
2 tsp. Accent- optional
2 Tbs. olive oil
1 32 oz. jar spaghetti sauce
1 pint small curd cottage cheese-Try low fat
4 Tbs. grated Parmesan cheese

    Sprinkle Accent over meat and brown
in oil. Layer ½ of noodles, meat and sauce
in 8 x 11½ x 2 casserole. Top with pint of
cottage cheese. Repeat layers of noodles,
meat and sauce. Sprinkle with cheese
and bake in a 375° oven for 30 minutes.

Garlic Bread

Slice one loaf Italian bread in one inch slices, not cutting through bottom. Mix 1 stick softened butter with 1/2 tsp. garlic powder and 1 Tbs. parsley. Spread garlic butter over top of loaf and be- tween slices. Wrap loaf in foil and heat in 350° oven for 15 minutes while lasagna is cooking. Serve bread in cute basket with napkin in it.

Delicious breadsticks are usually available at your favorite Italian restaurant. Call and arrange to have them ready if time is short.

Tutti - Frutti Tortoni

Soften 1 quart vanilla ice cream. Add ½ cup chopped candied fruit, ½ cup chopped raisins and 1 ½ tsp. rum flavoring. Spoon into 8 large paper bake cups. Set in muffin pan Freeze till nearly firm. Poke whole toasted almond in center of each, point down. Freeze firm. Remove from paper cups when ready to serve.

Menu for Brunch for the Bunch

Mimosa Punch
Company Strata
Curried Fruit Compote
Cinnamon Rolls and Bran Muffins

In golf as in life,
it's the follow-through that counts.

An expert is someone who can take something you already knew and make it

Happiness is Still Homemade

Brunch for the Bunch

21

Punch for the Bunch

Tangerine or orange juice - 2 quarts
1 46 ounce can unsweetened pineapple juice
1 quart club soda

   Chill juice and combine with club soda in large container. Pour into punch bowl or pitcher. This is very pretty served with an ice mold in the punch bowl. Make the mold from orange slices and mint leaves. Allow several hours for mold to freeze.

Nothing makes you more tolerant of a neighbor's party than being invited.

Laughter is a tranquilizer with no side effects.

Company Strata   *Must be made ahead*
Feed to birds

Remove crust from 12 slices of bread
Cut out 12 donuts and holes with a donut cutter
from the bread. Cut each piece of bread into
4 strips if you don't have a donut cutter.

Fit the leftover scraps in bottom of 13x9x2
baking dish.

Layer 12 oz. sharp process cheese slices, one
10 oz. package frozen chopped broccoli, cooked
and drained and 2 cups diced cooked ham
or chicken over bread.

Arrange donuts and holes on top.

Combine 6 slightly beaten eggs, 3 1/2 cups
milk, 2 Tbs. instant minced onion, 1/2 tsp. salt
and 1/4 tsp. dry mustard. Pour over donuts
and holes. Cover and refrigerate 6 hours or
overnight. Let come to room temperature.
Bake uncovered in 350° oven for 1 hour. Let
stand 20 minutes for the custard to set up.
Serves 10.

23

Curried Fruit Compote.

Make the day before and bake in the oven with strata.

1 large can pineapple chunks
1 large can pear halves
1 large can apricots
1 small jar cherries (Maraschino)
1 stick of butter, melted
3/4 cup brown sugar
1 tsp. curry, optional

Drain fruit well. Cut pears into quarters. Arrange in baking dish with a row of each fruit with pears in center row. Put a cherry in center of each pear. Pour melted butter on top. Mix sugar and curry. Sprinkle over fruit. Bake at 325° for 1 hour. Serves 10.

24

Hot Buns and Muffins

Frozen cinnamon swirl buns and muffins are hard to beat! Spray kitchen with cinnamon spray or sprinkle cinnamon on top of stove and turn on burner at low heat. Smells great through the house.

Menu for Dinner at Eight

Elegant caviar
Date-cheese ball
Standing rib roast
Yorkshire pudding
Broccoli casserole
Marvelous rice
Chutney peaches
Rolls
Coconut ice cream balls with chocolate
   sauce

When serving food, always serve from
your guests' left and remove from the
right. Water and other beverages are
served on the right

Dinner at Eight

Simply Elegant Caviar

Take a pretty bowl, plop in a pint of sour cream. Chop one small onion. Spread over sour cream. Top with small jar of black caviar. Serve with crackers or bread, toasted very dry with crusts removed.

Always forgive your enemies; Nothing annoys them so much.

The problem is not the problem. The problem is my attitude about the problem.

Date Cheese Ball

2 8 oz. packages "Light" cream cheese
2 Tbs. low fat milk
½ cup chopped walnuts or pecans
8 oz. chopped dates (not sugar-coated)

Process in food processor, mixer or blender until evenly mixed. Add another tablespoon of milk if it looks too stiff. Shape into ball and garnish with grapes and nuts. This is delicious served with Norwegian Flat Breads.

Yorkshire Pudding. *Be brave—see how simple it is.*

In medium bowl, mix 1 cup all purpose flour and 1 tsp. salt. Slowly stir in 1 cup milk. Add 2 eggs, one at a time. Beat together until smooth. (You can do this in a blender.) Can be refrigerated 2 hours so make earlier. Remove roast from oven. Increase oven temperature to 425°. Spoon 1 tsp. drippings from roast into each of 12 muffin pan cups or 1/4 cup drippings into 9" square pan. Set pan in oven until fat is very hot, about 5 minutes. Stir batter. Fill each muffin tin 2/3 full or pour all batter into 9" pan. Bake 25 to 30 minutes. *Your guests will be impressed!*

Delicious Standing Rib Roast

1 standing beef rib roast 7 to 9 lbs.

2 tsp. salt, 1 tsp. garlic powder, 1/4 tsp. pepper

Preheat oven to 325°. Place beef, fat side up, on rack in open roasting pan. Sprinkle with salt, garlic powder and pepper. Allow 23 to 25 minutes per pound for rare, 27 to 30 minutes for medium, 32 to 35 for well done. For easier carving, remove roast from oven and let stand 20 to 30 minutes. Now go ahead, be brave and make the easy Yorkshire pudding.

Horseradish sauce to pass with the roast.
1 1/3 cups sour cream, 3 tablespoons horseradish and 1 tsp. prepared mustard. Mix well. Delicious with ham too.

Chutney Peaches. *Colorful and delicious!*

Canned peach halves - ½ peach per person
1 bottle mango chutney or mincemeat

Drain peach halves and place cut side up in flat casserole dish. Fill center with chutney or sauce and bake at 350° for 15 minutes.

This is a perfect dish for the microwave. Whole cranberry sauce works well too for a filling.

If you want to gather honey, don't kick over the bee hive.

Marvelous Rice

½ cup butter
1 medium onion, chopped
1 lb. fresh mushrooms, sliced   *-You can use the ones from a jar.*
2 cups rice
2 8 oz. cans undiluted consommé
3 cups water

Melt butter in a heavy skillet. Saute onions and mushrooms 5 minutes. Set aside. Rinse rice off and drain well. Place rice in skillet in which onions and mushrooms were sautéed. Brown rice and add consommé and water. Add mushrooms and onions. Bring to a boil. Cover and simmer about 25 minutes until liquid is absorbed and rice is tender. Serves 8.

33

"Better than Broccoli" Casserole

2 packages chopped frozen broccoli
1 cup grated cheddar cheese
14 Ritz crackers, crushed
scant cup of mayonaise
2 eggs, well beaten
1 can cream of mushroom soup
3 Tbs. butter

   Cook broccoli 5 minutes and drain. Mix with cheese, mayonaise, eggs and soup. Put in greased casserole and sprinkle with cracker crumbs. Dot with butter. Bake at 350° for 30 minutes. Serves 8.

Coconut Ice Cream Balls

½ gallon vanilla ice cream
2 cups grated coconut
a jar of good hot fudge sauce

Make ice cream balls in advance, using a scoop. Roll in coconut, place on a cookie sheet and place in freezer until ready to serve. Looks beautiful in sherbert glasses.

Pour syrup over ice cream balls but for a more gourmet taste, use Kahlua instead of chocolate syrup.

Some Things Never to Do

1. Don't apologize for your cooking ability or the quality of your cuisine. Some people have the means to take friends to the most expensive restaurants, but gracious hospitality in your own home surpasses unlimited expense accounts.

2. Don't undertake the unattainable. Plan a reasonable menu that you can serve effortlessly. Allow enough time. Don't try to do all the tasks the day of the party.

3. If food or drink is refused, never make an issue out of it. Respect their willpower.

4. Never make a big deal over spills, breaks or accidents at your party. Clean it up quickly and quietly. The guests will feel much better if you don't look upset all evening.

The test of good manners is to be able to put up pleasantly with bad ones.

Big secret! Don't worry about fresh flowers if they're not available. Use fake flowers with __real__ greenery. They can be paper, silk, etc.

Be sure to put water in your bowl.

Make sure the height of your centerpiece remains below eye level if guests are seated.

You can use candlesticks during the day but don't light the candles.

Menu for a Luncheon for Lovely Ladies

1. Polynesian chicken salad

2. Curried chicken deluxe

3. Crab Louis

Serve with a ring of veggies - carrot curls, radish rosettes, parsley.

Use small butter rolls with strawberry butter.

Wow 'em with "potted ice cream with daisies."

The definition of chaos is six women dividing one luncheon check.

38

Luncheons for Lovely Ladies

39

Polynesian Chicken Salad *Deluxe!*

3 cups cooked chicken cut into bite size pieces

   Always use a fryer for this. Simmer chicken for 1 hour in water seasoned with 1 onion quartered, 2 stalks celery, 1 carrot quartered, salt and pepper.

1 cup diced canned pineapple or diced apple or seedless grapes.

3/4 cup toasted almonds, slivered

1/2 cup mayonnaise

1/4 cup sour cream

1 cup diced celery, 1/2 tsp. salt and pepper, 2 Tbs. lemon juice

   Sprinkle cut up cooked chicken with lemon juice. Let stand 1 hour then combine all ingredients and chill. Put salad on shredded lettuce in center of plate and ring with cucumber slices, carrot curls, radish rosettes, and curly endive. Serves 6.

40

Curried Chicken Salad *Excellent!*

3 cups chicken, cooked and cubed
2 tsp. curry powder
2 tsp onion, chopped
2 Tbs. lemon juice - ½ tsp. salt and pepper
¼ cup toasted coconut ⎫
¼ cup chutney ⎬ *plus enough to garnish each salad*
¼ cup golden raisins ⎭
½ cup mayonnaise - ½ cup sour cream

Simmer fryer 1 hour in water seasoned with 1 onion, quartered, 2 stalks celery, 1 carrot quartered, salt + pepper. Sprinkle cut up chicken with lemon juice. Let stand 1 hour. Combine all ingredients except garnish and chill. Garnish with a sprinkling of toasted coconut and raisins. Serves 6

41

Crab Louis - *elegant and easy and expensive*

1 ½ lbs. crabmeat
shredded lettuce
6 tomatoes
6 hard cooked eggs
1 avocado
Crab Louis sauce

Get as large pieces of crab as possible. Check crab carefully to remove all shell. On each of 6 salad plates arrange a bed of lettuce. In center of each, place a mound of crabmeat. Surround with wedges of tomatoes, hard cooked eggs and avocado. Serve well chilled with the following sauce.

42

Crab Louis Sauce

1 cup mayonaise
2 Tbs. grated onion
1 Tbs. lemon juice
1 tsp. minced green pepper
½ cup chili sauce
1 tsp. Worcestershire
dash of Cayenne pepper
salt and pepper to taste.

Mix well and chill. When ready to serve, pour over crab meat.

A nice touch is to give each guest their own individual sauce cup made from a hollowed out lemon shell.

43

Strawberry Butter

Mix a carton of whipped, unsalted butter with a jar of strawberry preserves.

Cream Cheese - Jam Spread

Spoon strawberry jam over a block of Neufchatel or cream cheese.

Serve either one as a fabulous spread for hot rolls, bagels, warm muffins. What a treat!

Tips to Destine Your Party for Success.

Don't settle for the usual. Be different! No, not necessarily with gourmet food or expensive floral arrangements but with unique touches and a very gracious attitude.

Themes make parties easier. Choose one and start thinking creatively. Carry the theme out with your centerpiece, favors and something special at the door. Tie balloons on your mailbox so your guests know which house is yours. Keep on hand a plain grapevine wreath to hang on the door. Put on doves with lace ribbon for bridal festivities, a teddy bear for baby showers.

45

Ways to Make Your Guests Feel Welcome

In making your guests feel welcome, you are carrying out the principle behind entertaining; the desire to please someone in a personal way.

Cut the first piece of cheese and spread the first cracker to assist your guests and make them feel at ease.

Don't apologize for the size of your home, the way it's decorated or your cleaning abilities. Your friends are there to enjoy your hospitality and to socialize with your guests; not to criticize you. Also, it embarrasses your guests and makes them feel uncomfortable.

Don't forget; manners are the manifestation

Potted Ice Cream
Guaranteed Raves!

Try Pistachio ice cream with chocolate sprinkles or your favorite flavor with green tinted coconut for grass.

You will need a small clay pot for each person, clear straws to stick daisy through in center of ice cream. Clear plastic cups for liners for ice cream. Drop a scoop of ice cream into each pot with liner and stick a flower in the middle

How to have your own cookie swap

The things you need for a successful cookie exchange are a few cookie-loving friends and a place to gather.

Well in advance, set a date and send invitations to as many of your family and friends as you can accommodate. Ask each person you invite to bring 3 dozen of her favorite or special cookies.

You can ask your guests to bring their own containers or you can provide them. Have some small plastic bags for particular cookie swappers who don't like to mix varieties.

Try to bake an extra batch of cookies in case someone

48

The Cookie Swap 49

Iced Lemon Squares

The best of the rest with a delicious icing.

2 cups all-purpose flour
1 cup butter
1/2 cup powdered sugar
4 eggs
4 tablespoons lemon juice
2 teaspoons grated lemon rind
2 cups sugar
4 tablespoons all-purpose flour
1 teaspoon baking powder

Icing

3/4 cup powdered sugar
1 1/2 teaspoons vanilla extract
2 tablespoons butter, softened
1 tablespoon milk

Preheat oven to 350 degrees F.
Cream together flour, butter and powdered sugar. Press evenly into an ungreased 16 x 11 pan. Bake 20 minutes. Beat together eggs, lemon juice, lemon rind, sugar, flour and baking powder. Pour this mixture over baked first layer. Return to oven. Bake 25 minutes. Cool. For icing: Combine ingredients for icing and beat until smooth. Spread on lemon squares. Yields 36 squares

Melt in Your Mouth Reese's Candy Cookies
Elegant and easy!

1 package mini Reese's cup candy.
1 loaf Pillsbury peanut butter cookie dough

Cut dough into slices per package directions. Then cut each slice into fourths. Press a quartered slice into mini muffin pan. Bake according to package directions. As soon as you remove from oven, press peeled mini Reese's cup candy into each one. Excellent and easy!

Sugar Cookies

Great for little ones with cookie cutters in hand!

1 cup butter or margarine, softened
1½ cups granulated sugar
2 teaspoons vanilla extract
1 teaspoon almond extract
2 eggs
1 Tablespoon water
3 cups all-purpose flour
2 teaspoons baking powder
¼ teaspoon salt

Cream butter with sugar together in bowl. Add vanilla and almond extracts, eggs and water. Combine flour, baking powder and salt. and blend into creamed mixture. Refrigerate overnight if possible. Roll out for cutting on a floured surface. Brush tops with milk before sprinkling with sugar or decorations. Bake at 375 degrees F. for 8 to 10 minutes.

Oatmeal Crispies.

This dough needs to be chilled a day before baking.

1 cup solid vegetable shortening
1 cup light brown sugar
1 cup granulated sugar
2 eggs
1 ½ cups unsifted all-purpose flour
1 teaspoon salt
1 teaspoon baking soda
2 heaping cups quick-cooking oats
1½ cups raisins
1½ cups chopped pecans

Combine flour, salt and baking soda. Beat together shortening, sugars and vanilla until creamy. Add eggs, beating until light and fluffy. Gradually beat in flour mixture and oats. Stir in raisins and pecans. Shape into 5 or 6 long rolls; wrap each in waxed paper and chill thoroughly. (At least 6 hours but up to 2 days.) When ready to bake, preheat oven to 350 degrees. Slice cookies about ¼ inch thick. Bake on ungreased cookie sheet for 10 to 11 minutes. Makes 75 plus cookies.

⭐ Our Favorite Cookies ⭐

1 cup butter
1 cup sugar
1 cup brown sugar
1 egg
1 cup vegetable oil
1 teaspoon vanilla extract
1 cup regular rolled oats

1 cup crushed cornflakes
½ cup shredded coconut
½ cup chopped pecans
3½ cups sifted all-purpose flour
1 teaspoon baking soda
1 teaspoon salt

Preheat oven to 325 degrees F.
Cream butter and sugars until light and fluffy.
Add egg, oil and vanilla. Mix well. Add oats,
cornflakes, coconut and nuts. Stir well. Add
flour, soda and salt. Stir until well blended.
Drop by teaspoonfuls onto ungreased cookie
sheets. Flatten with fork dipped in water.
Bake 15 minutes. Cool on wire rack.
Yields 8 dozen. These freeze well.

Classic Chocolate Chip Cookies
and "Clinton Cookies"

2 ¼ cups all-purpose flour - (Only use 1 ½ cups flour
  if making "Clinton Cookies." Oats are in hers.)
1 teaspoon salt
1 teaspoon baking soda
1 cup solid vegetable shortening
½ cup granulated sugar
1 cup firmly packed light brown sugar
1 teaspoon vanilla extract
2 eggs
2 cups old-fashioned oats (for Clinton cookies only)
12 oz. pkg. semisweet chocolate chips

  Preheat oven to 350 degrees F. Combine flour,
salt and baking soda. Beat together shortening,
sugars and vanilla until creamy. Add eggs, beating until light and fluffy. Gradually beat in
flour mixture (plus 2 cups rolled oats for "Hillary
Clinton" cookies.) Stir in chocolate chips. Drop
batter by well rounded teaspoonfuls onto ungreased cookie sheets. Bake 8 to 10 minutes or
until cookies are done. Cool cookies on sheets
for 2 minutes before placing them on wire racks. 55

Menu for a Mexican Fiesta

Queso Dip with Taco Chips

Refried Bean Dip

Guacamole Salad

Mexican Chicken

Cheesy Cornbread

Sangria

Traditional Flan

It's not the size of the dog in the fight,
But the size of the fight in the dog

58

Mexican Fiesta

Mexican Queso Dip

1 lb. mild Cheddar cheese, grated

1 4 oz. can green chili peppers, drained and chopped

1 egg

2 Tbs. milk

Place cheese in a 9" pan. Place chilies on top. Mix egg and milk in bowl and pour over chilies. Bake at 425° for 40 minutes. Serve with taco chips. Serves 6 to 8.

Refried Bean Dip

1 12 oz. jar mild Picante Salsa
1 16 oz. can plain refried beans
1 cup shredded cheddar cheese
½ pint sour cream

Mix Picante Salsa and refried beans together. Put into pretty pie or quiche dish. Sprinkle cheese over top. Heat in 350° oven till cheese melts. Decorate with big scoops of sour cream.
Serve with taco chips.

Guacamole Salad

On bed of lettuce, lay slices of avocado, sprinkle with lemon juice, diced tomato. Garnish with minced, cooked bacon or "Real bacon bits" from the jar. Pour store-bought taco salad dressing over salad.

Suggestion: to ripen avocado or tomato quickly place it into a brown paper bag and store in a dark place. - works with bananas too. *Fruit ripens 5 times faster when stored with other fruit.*

60

Set the mood with music, a piñata for the centerpiece, a sheet for the tablecloth, bright colored finger-tip towels for napkins.

61

Mexican Chicken Casserole

1 cut up fryer or 6 half breasts
1 medium onion, chopped - 2 Tbs. butter
1 can cream of celery soup
1 can cream of chicken soup
1 can tomatoes - 1 tsp. Tabasco
1 package Doritos - 2 4oz. chopped green chilies
1 1/2 cups grated sharp cheddar cheese

Simmer chicken 1 hour in water seasoned with 1 onion, 2 stalks celery, salt and pepper. Remove from bones and cut in bite size pieces. Saute onion in butter. Add soups, tomatoes, Tabasco and green chilies. Heat thoroughly. Spread Doritos over bottom of 9 x 13 x 2 greased casserole. Place chicken on top. Pour sauce over all.

Mexican Corn Bread

Ballard corn bread mix

1 egg

4 pieces bacon, cooked

6 green onions, chopped

6 oz. cheddar cheese, grated

Jalapeno peppers to taste-seeds removed

1 small can cream style corn

Follow directions on corn bread mix box, plus extra egg, chopped bacon, onion, cheese, peppers and corn added to batter. Heat iron skillet with 1 Tbs. oil in it while oven is pre-heating. Bake at 425° 15 to 20 minutes.

Non-alcoholic Sangria punch

1 26 oz. bottle of grape juice (not white)
1 28 oz. bottle of tonic water
½ cup sugar
1 sliced orange
1 sliced lemon
1 sliced peach

Combine all ingredients and mix well. Serve cold in a pretty pitcher.

Good examples have twice the value of good advice.

No act of kindness is ever lost; it becomes a part of all the lives

Believe me it's simple, Flan

4 Tbs. brown sugar
3 eggs, slightly beaten
1 cup evaporated milk
2/3 cup water
1/3 cup sugar
1 1/2 tsp. vanilla
1/4 tsp. salt

Preheat oven to 350°. Lightly press 1 Tbs. brown sugar into each of 4 custard cups. Combine remaining ingredients in large bowl and mix well. Carefully pour into custard cups. Set cups into shallow pan. Add 1 inch water to pan. Bake 50 minutes or until set. (A knife inserted into center of custard will come out clean.) Loosen edges with knife and unmold on individual serving plates. Serves 4.

Menu for a Midnight Repast

Invite friends over for a light supper after the theater, art show, movie or concert.

Crock of cheese with assorted crackers

Caesar salad

Snow's New England clam chowder

Some wonderful breads and butter

Delicious pecan pie

Very easy, always available, ice cream pie

The man who does nothing but wait for his ship to come in has already missed the boat.

66

A Midnight Repast

Caesar Salad

2 heads romaine lettuce, washed, dried and torn into bite size pieces.

2 cups packaged garlic croutons

½ cup freshly grated Parmesan cheese

Dressing

Combine ¼ cup creamy Caesar dressing with ¼ cup regular Caesar dressing

1 can (2oz.) anchovy fillets, chopped (optional)

In large salad bowl, toss greens with dressing. Sprinkle on cheese and croutons. Toss again lightly. Makes 8 servings.

You don't have to get up early to make this homemade bread!!

I unsliced loaf from the bakery
1 egg
a sprinkle of sesame seeds or dill.

brush loaf with egg drop seeds over top. Wrap in foil leaving top open. Bake in 350° till hot- 10 to 15 minutes.

69

Delicious Pecan Pie   *So simple - no crust to make.*

3 egg whites, stiffly beaten
1/8 tsp. cream of tartar
1 cup sugar
1 tsp. baking powder
1 cup chopped pecans or macadamia nuts
1 cup graham cracker crumbs
1 carton Cool Whip or ice cream for garnish

Beat egg whites with cream of tartar till very stiff. Fold in next 4 ingredients gently by hand. Pour into ungreased 9" glass pie plate. Bake at 325° for 25 minutes. This is better made a day ahead.

Very, Very Easy Ice Cream Pie

Fill a bought chocolate cookie crust with softened ice cream - your favorite kind. Freeze. When ready to serve, slice and pour a jar of hot fudge sauce (warmed) over pie. *These ingredients are easy to keep on hand for when unexpected guests drop in.*

Failure isn't fatal and success isn't final.

A closed mind is a stuffy place! 71

Menu for Old Fashioned Picnic

Fried chicken - yours or theirs

Classic potato salad

Baked beans

Deviled eggs

Carrot sticks, olives, celery

Mysterious cookies + brownies -

Love is like the five loaves and two fishes. It doesn't start to multiply until you give it away

Be sure you invite Duncan Hines - he makes wonderful brownies!

An Old Fashioned Picnic

73

Baked Beans the easy but delicious way.

2 1 lb. 12 oz. can pork and beans *B&M's are super.*

½ cup dark brown sugar

2 tsp. dry mustard

1 cup chopped onions

½ cup molasses

1 cup ketchup or chili sauce

¼ cup Worcestershire sauce

5 strips bacon, chopped in small pieces

2 Tbs. liquid smoke

Mix all ingredients together. Bake in large

Visit your local flea or basket market for baskets. They are perfect for decorating and picnics.

Joe's Flea Market

SALE
BASKETS
TODAY ONLY

75

Classic Deviled Eggs

6 hard cooked eggs cut in half, lengthwise. Remove yolks carefully and mash with fork or put through a fine strainer. Set whites aside. Add 1 tsp salt, 1 tsp. dry mustard and 1 1/2 Tbs. mayonnaise to yolks. Mash to a smooth paste; if too stiff add a little more mayonnaise. Cut thin slice off bottom of egg white half to make it lie flat. Fill the egg white with yolk mixture using a pastry tube or spoon. Garnish with paprika. Chill before serving.

How to make perfect hard cooked eggs
Place eggs in saucepan in a single layer; cover with cold water. Bring to just under a boil. Turn off heat; cover and let stand 15 minutes. Drain and immerse in cold water to stop cooking. Refrigerate- *No more green yolks!*

Two can live as cheaply as one –
If one doesn't eat.

The real test in golf and in life,
is not keeping out of the rough,
but in getting out after we are in. 77

How to cook perfect crispy fried chicken.

Remove the skin from a fryer if you choose. You should choose to for your health's sake. Soak chicken in water then quickly put it in a paper bag with 2 cups flour and shake till chicken is totally coated. Remove the chicken and lay it on a piece of wax paper. Leave it there for <u>at least 30 minutes.</u> This will form a seal and will look as if you put glue on the chicken. This odd looking batter will form a coating on the chicken that seals the juices in and keeps the grease out when frying. Place your chicken in hot shortening about 1 inch deep and immediately put lid on your deep, heavy cast iron skillet. Cook on medium heat—never too fast or it will get brown on the outside before the inside cooks. When the chicken is brown on one side, turn each piece over <u>once only.</u> Turning chicken more than once makes it greasy. Cook about 12 minutes on each side. If you put a few drops of yellow food coloring in the shortening <u>after</u> the shortening heats, it will give your chicken the most beautiful color

Carrot-walnut muffins
Blueberry muffins
Buy a good brand of frozen muffins.
Heat as suggested - pull out of
paper cups and put in your
own basket with pretty napkin...
and don't tell your secret.

Give a little boy enough rope
and he will come home with
a stray dog at the end of it.

Classic Potato Salad

8 large potatoes
1/4 cup chopped onions
1 cup chopped celery
6 hard-boiled eggs, chopped
1 cup mayonnaise

4 Tbs. vinegar
1 Tbs. prepared mustard
1 pinch of sugar
salt and pepper to taste
1 tsp. Beau Monde

Boil potatoes in jackets until tender. Peel and cube. Sprinkle vinegar over hot potatoes. Toss. Let cool. Combine remaining ingredients and add to potatoes. Toss well. Chill. Sprinkle paprika on top.

God sends food for the birds but He doesn't throw it in the nest.

Pecan-Toffee Cookies
Simply delicious!

24 graham crackers
2 sticks butter or margarine
1 cup brown sugar
1 cup chopped pecans
   or sliced almonds
   Preheat oven to 350°F.
Place the crackers over
a cookie sheet. In sauce-
pan, melt butter; then stir
in sugar. Bring to a boil
and stir for 3 minutes.
Pour evenly over the crackers. Now spread
the nuts over crackers. Bake 10 minutes.
Cool 10 minutes and cut into bars.

81

Menu   for Ballgames and Black-eyed Peas
Hopping John
Glazed Ham with pickled peaches
Italian Cole Slaw
Cornbread
Tunnel of fudge cupcakes

People who don't know it they're coming
or going are usually in the biggest hurry
to get there.

A good friend doubles the joy
and divides the pain.

Ballgames and Black-eyed Peas

Hopping John

Start the New Year out right with this traditional dish!

1 cup white rice   or 3/4 cup brown rice

6 strips of bacon   or Sizzlean

1 onion, chopped

2 10 oz. packages frozen black-eyed peas

1/8 tsp. Tabasco

3 1/2 cups water

1 bouillon cube - chicken or beef

salt and pepper to taste

Dice bacon into deep sauce pan; add onions and saute over medium heat until onion is tender. Add peas and rice, then water. Cover and simmer over low heat about 45 minutes. Salt and pepper to taste. Many people add 2 1 lb. cans of tomatoes. *Delicious!*

84

Glazed Ham with Pickled Peaches

Buy a boneless and fully cooked ham (the amount depends on the crowd.) Place ham on rack in shallow baking pan. Do not cover or add water. Heat in slow oven, 325° according to directions on wrapper. Half an hour before time is up, spoon marmalade glaze over ham. Continue heating 30 minutes more, spooning glaze over 2 to 3 times.

Marmalade glaze: to a small jar of orange marmalade or apricot preserves add enough syrup from a jar of spiced pickled peaches to make a glaze consistency. For garnish, make slices from 2 or 3 of the pickled peaches and put on top of the ham, pegged on by whole cloves. Put the rest of the peaches around ham.

85

Italian Style Slaw - *Keeps a long time in fridge.*
Shred 1 head of cabbage and 1 large onion.
Layer in bowl. Pour ¾ cup sugar over top.
Bring these ingredients to boil:
1 cup vinegar
¾ cup salad oil
1 tsp. salt
1 tsp. dry mustard
1 tsp. celery seed

Pour above over cabbage and onion while still
hot. Let stand at room temperature to cool
then refrigerate.

Sour cream corn bread. *So moist it tastes like cake.*

½ cup cooking oil

1   8½ oz. can cream style corn

1 cup sour cream

1 cup self-rising corn meal

2 eggs

1 tsp. salt

pinch of sugar (optional)

Mix all together. Bake in 9" pie pan or skillet or muffin tins. Bake at 400° for 25 to 30 minutes.

We always have time for the things we put first.

87

Tunnel of fudge + cream cheese cupcake. *Sounds hard—very easy.*

1 (2 layer) package chocolate cake mix

1 8 oz. package cream cheese, softened

1/3 cup sugar

1 egg

dash of salt

1 6 oz. package semi-sweet chocolate chips

Mix cake by directions on box. Fill paper lined muffin tins 2/3 full. Cream cheese with sugar; now beat in salt and egg. Stir in chocolate chips. Drop 1 rounded teaspoon cheese mixture into each cupcake. Bake by package directions for cupcakes - usually 350°, 15 to 20 minutes.

Creative Ways to Serve Food

Arrange veggies on a full head of cauliflower with leaves still attached. Stud the cauliflower with vegetables on toothpicks. Keep an extra supply in the fridge to replenish the arrangement.

Use endive and small cherry tomatoes for a colorful, textured fringe around meat.

Serve dips in round unsliced loaves of pumpernickel bread or make a bowl from a hollowed out red cabbage.

Shrimp cocktail sauce is especially beautiful in a hollowed-out lemon shell. Cut bottom off so it will sit straight and zig-zag the edges. For individual servings.

For a memorable breakfast, serve each guest their own tiny plate or cup of jelly or jam.

Winning Desserts

Pistachio Dream Dessert

Butterscotch Torte

Strawberry Pie

Heavenly Ice Cream Pie

Triple Chocolate Cake

Banana - Chocolate Chip Cake

Try to serve desserts on an elevated cake plate - very pretty!

The trouble with trouble
Is that it starts out as fun.

Winning Desserts

Pistachio Dream Dessert - great looking and tasting! Makes 2 - keep one and share one.

50 Ritz crackers, crushed
1 stick butter, softened
3/4 cup coconut
1 quart vanilla ice cream
2 3oz packages instant pistachio pudding
1½ cup milk
12 oz. carton of Cool Whip

Mix crushed crackers and butter together and pat into 2 8x11½x2 casseroles. Bake 10 minutes at 350° in preheated oven. Cool. Toast 3/4 cup coconut till brown. Set aside for garnish. Soften 1 quart vanilla ice cream. Mix 2 3oz. packages of pudding with 1½ cups milk in large mixing bowl. Add ice cream and Cool Whip. Beat again. Spread over cooled crust. Garnish. Refrigerate

Some hints to help your guests feel welcome.

Good manners are simply a matter of common courtesy and consideration for other people. The minute friends arrive, make them feel comfortable, welcome, pampered and special.

Anticipate their needs. Sprinkle your home with thoughtfulness. Have a pencil and pad by the telephone for your guests and matches and ashtrays for those who insist.

Right before they arrive, take a quick peep at your bathroom. Be sure there is fresh soap, a new roll of toilet tissue, facial tissue and clean guest towels. Pretty paper ones are fine; then they won't feel guilty about using the fancy ones. Put a flower in a small vase and light a scented candle.

Butterscotch Torte - *Can be made with chocolate.*

Step 1- 1 cup all purpose flour

   1 stick butter, melted

   1 cup chopped pecans

Mix and spread in 10" spring pan. Bake 15 minutes at 325°

Step 2 - 8 oz. softened cream cheese

   1 cup powdered sugar

   1 cup Cool Whip from 12 oz. container

Mix creamed cheese and sugar. Fold in Cool Whip
Spread over crust.

Step 3 - 2 boxes Butterscotch pudding mix

   3 cups milk - Make according to directions
on box using only 3 cups milk. Spread over cheese
mixture after it's cool. Spread Cool Whip over that.

Beautiful Strawberry Pie

1 cup sugar

1 cup water- *try substituting 7 Up. It's even better.*

4 Tbs. cornstarch

3 Tbs. strawberry gelatin

1 quart strawberries

1 baked pie shell

   Combine sugar, water and cornstarch. Boil 5 minutes till thick. Add 3 Tbs. gelatin and a few drops red food coloring. Stir till dissolved. Place strawberries in baked pie shell, point end up. Pour liquid over strawberries. Chill. Garnish with whipped cream.

How to make perfect meringue

3 egg whites - ¼ tsp. cream of tartar
½ tsp. vanilla - 6 Tbs. sugar

Have egg whites at room temperature. (They will whip fluffier.) Be sure your bowl and beaters are <u>very</u> clean (or they will not whip fluffier.) Beat egg whites with cream of tartar till foamy and soft peaks form. <u>Gradually</u> add sugar beating till stiff and glossy; then add vanilla. Spread meringue over pie filling that is at room temperature, sealing meringue to edges of pie crust. This prevents shrinking. Bake at 350° 12 to 15 minutes. Makes an 8" or 9" pie.

'96

Absolutely Heavenly Ice Cream Pie

<u>The coconut crust</u>: Mix 2 cups Baker's Angel Flake coconut and ¼ cup melted butter. Press into an 8" or 9" inch pie pan. Bake at 300° until brown - 30 to 35 minutes. The <u>filling</u>: Pack 2 to 3 pints ice cream into crust. Butter pecan, coffee or vanilla are great. Ripple with a jar of good chocolate sauce. Freeze till firm. <u>The topping</u>: Beat 3 egg whites with ¼ tsp. cream of tartar till foamy and soft peaks form. Gradually add 6 Tbs. sugar, beating till stiff and glossy and all sugar is dissolved. Add ½ tsp. vanilla. Spread meringue over filling, sealing to crust. Sprinkle with ⅔ cup coconut. Place pie on a board. Bake at 500° until lightly browned; about 2 minutes. Can be frozen. *I use an old cutting board.*

Triple Chocolate Cake - *Fabulous!*

1 package devil's food cake mix
1 package (4 servings) instant chocolate pudding mix
1 cup sour cream
1/2 cup cooking oil
1/2 cup brewed coffee
1/2 cup Kahlua or dark rum
4 large eggs
2 cups semi-sweet chocolate chips

Combine all ingredients except chocolate chips in the bowl of your electric mixer. Mix on low to blend. Beat at medium speed for 1 minutes. Scrape the sides of bowl then beat 1 minute more. Fold in chocolate chips. Pour into well-greased, floured Bundt pan. Bake at 350°for 40 minutes to 1 hour, until cake springs back when touched.

Cool in pan on rack for 1/2 hour. Turn out gently on serving plate. Sit atand overnight foe chocolate chips to firm up.

98

Banana - Chocolate Chip Cake -

3/4 cup butter or margarine

1½ cup sugar

2 eggs

1 tsp. salt

1 cup mashed bananas

½ cup buttermilk or ½ cup sweet milk with 1 Tbs. vinegar.

1 tsp. baking powder

1 tsp. soda

2 cups all purpose flour.

1 small package chocolate chips

Glaze - Cream ¼ cup butter, 1 box confectioners sugar ¼ cup milk 1 tsp. vanilla or lemon flavoring.

Spoon glaze over cake.

Cream butter and sugar. Add eggs. Beat. Mix in bananas milk, salt, baking powder, soda and flour. Beat 1 minute more. Fold in chocolate chips. Bake 1 hour at 350° in greased tube pan. Let cool on rack 30 minutes

99

Doctors tell you that if you eat plenty, you will eat less. This is particularly true if you are a member of a large family.

Classics for Family Gatherings
Smoked turkey
Pot roast
Sweet potato balls
Cranberry salad mold
Asparagus and peas casserole
Carrot Cake

Family Gatherings

101

How to make perfect baked potatoes

Idaho baking potatoes - 1 per person

Preheat oven to 425°. Wash, dry and rub with salad oil. Do <u>not</u> wrap in foil. (They will steam instead of bake and will not be flaky.) Bake 45 to 60 minutes, depending on size. When potatoes are half done, pull out rack, quickly prick potato skin once with fork permitting steam to escape. When done, remove from oven and cut 1½ inch cross on top of each. Press until fluffy white of potato bursts through the opening. Pass bowls of butter, sour cream, snipped chives (frozen food department) and crisp bacon crumbled. You can use the kind in a jar.

102

Rules for Perfect Rice

To keep rice white when cooking in hard water, add 1 tablespoon vinegar to the cooking water.

One cup raw rice equals 3½ cups when cooked.

Fluffy boiled rice - Bring to a rolling boil: 2 cups water or stock. Add ¾ teaspoon salt and slowly stir 1 cup white or brown rice into water so as not to disturb the boiling. Cover and cook over slow heat. White rice will take 20 minutes, brown rice 45. Do not stir or lift cover. Turn off heat and allow rice to steam, covered, for an additional 10 minutes.

Yellow rice - Great with curry - Make the same as white rice above only add 15 grains saffron to the boiling water.

Peas and Asparagus Casserole · Easy & do ahead

1 large (17 oz.) can Le Sueur peas
2 large (15 oz.) can asparagus
3 chopped hard boiled eggs
1 ½ cans mushroom soup
6 oz. sharp Cheddar cheese

Layer in ungreased casserole in order listed. Top with grated cheese. Bake uncovered at 350° for 30 minutes. Serves 8.

Love is very much like eating a mushroom: You never know if it's the real thing until it's too late.

Sunday Best Round Bone Pot Roast

Rinse roast with water and pat dry. Salt and pepper to taste. Dust with garlic powder. Pour 1 Tbs. cooking oil in bottom of dutch oven. (A heavy pot with a lid) Brown both sides well. Cover immediately and turn heat down to very low. Cook 3 hours, then put potatoes and carrots around roast. You may have to add 1 cup of water at this time. Cook till quartered vegetables are tender - about 30 to 40 minutes.

There is no limit to what can be accomplished if it doesn't matter who gets the credit.

How to make perfect gelatin molds.

1- Spray the mold lightly with Pam spray.

2- To keep fruit evenly dispersed and prevent it from floating in the mold, cool gelatin, until it just begins to gel and is the consistency of thick egg white. Then stir in fruit.

3- To unmold gelatin, just loosen the edges from the pan with a knife. Dip mold up to its rim in warm, <u>not</u> hot water for a few seconds. Shake mold slightly so air can loosen gelatin. Invert a platter on top of mold; turn mold and platter over gently.

106

Cranberry Congealed Salad

Perfect for Thanksgiving.

1 3 oz. package cherry gelatin

1 3 oz. package lemon gelatin

1 cup boiling water

juice and grated rind of 1 orange

juice of 1 lemon

1 large can crushed pineapple, drained

1 can whole cranberry sauce

1 cup chopped pecans

Dissolve the gelatins in 1 cup boiling water. Add all other ingredients. Congeal in pretty mold.

107

Cream Chicken gravy - *See chicken under Beans.*

2 Tbs. oil
2 Tbs. flour
1 cup milk
salt and pepper

Pour all but about 2 tablespoons of the oil from the skillet you just fried your chicken in. Add the flour and stir over medium heat with a wooden spoon, scraping the pan until the mixture is blended and beginning to brown. Add the milk, salt and pepper and stir till thickened

Oven-Smoked Turkey

This turkey, roasted in a paper bag, has a marvelous smoked flavor.

1 10-12 pound turkey
¼ cup vegetable oil
4 Tbs. seasoned salt
¼ tsp. garlic powder
4 Tbs. liquid smoke
2 Tbs. freshly ground black pepper

Grease a large brown-paper grocery bag well with vegetable oil and set aside.

Preheat oven to 350°. Wash the turkey and pat dry with paper towels. Combine the ¼ cup vegetable oil, seasoned salt, garlic powder, liquid smoke and black pepper and mix together to make a paste. Rub the turkey well with the paste, inside and out. Place the turkey in the greased bag and tie the end closed with a piece of string. Place on a baking sheet and roast at 350° for 3½ hours. Remove from the oven and let stand at room temperature for at least 30 minutes before untying the bag and removing the turkey.

109

Sweet Potato Surprise Balls or Casserole

1 2 lb. 8 oz. can yams or 3 cups cooked, mashed
sweet potatoes.
3 Tbs. melted butter
1/3 cup sugar
1/2 cup chopped pecans or 1 cup coconut
1/2 tsp. salt
1/2 tsp. maple flavoring
1 egg, slightly beaten
8 marshmallows
crushed cornflakes

Season yams with salt, maple flavoring; add butter, sugar, egg and nuts or coconut. Beat well. Mold into a ball around each marshmallow. Roll in crushed cornflakes. Bake at 350° for 25 min. on greased pan.

For casserole, instead of making ball around each marshmallow, put in baking dish and put marshmallows on top the last 5 minutes of the 25 minute baking time.

110

"Special Touch" Carrot Cake.

2 cups sugar
2 cups self rising flour
1 tsp. cloves
2 tsp cinnamon
1½ cup salad oil
4 eggs
3 cups grated carrots
1 cup chopped pecans

Frosting

1 8 oz. pkg. cream cheese
1 stick softened butter
1 box confectioners sugar
1 tsp. vanilla
Cream together and frost cake. Garnish with rim of pecan or pistachio nuts.

Grate the carrots first. Grease and flour 3 8" layer cake pans. Sift together dry ingredients into your largest mixing bowl. Blend oil in. Add eggs, one at a time, beating well after each addition. Stir in grated carrots and nuts. Divide batter into 3 pans. Bake 350° for 25 minutes. Cool before frosting.

111

New Years Day Buffet Menu

Fresh Veggies and Dip
Crispy Party Mix
Sub Sandwiches
Italian Cole Slaw - *check Ballgames + Black-eyed Peas*
Potato Chips
Oreo Ice Cream Sandwiches

If you have to do wrong to be on the team,
You're on the wrong team.

New Year's Day Buffet   113

Call your favorite
deli or sub shop
and have them
deliver your favorite
sub.
A 4 foot sub feeds 22
A 5 foot sub feeds 26-28
A 6 foot sub feeds 32-34

Set sub sandwich in center of table...
It usually comes on a board.
Decorate with flags that say "Happy New Year."

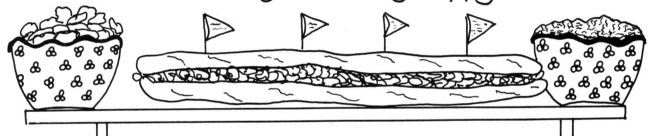

Put cole slaw and potato chips
in unusual bowls. If laundress
is celebrating too, use paper
napkins.... paper plates too.

Crispy Party Mix

3 Tbs. butter

1 tsp. seasoned salt

1/4 tsp. garlic powder (optional)

2 tsp. lemon juice

4 tsp. Worcestershire sauce

6 cups Crispix cereal

1 cup small round pretzels

1 cup salted mixed nuts

Melt butter in 13 x 9 x 2 pan in oven at 250°. Remove from oven. Add all ingredients, stirring till cereal is coated. Bake at 250° for 45 minutes, stirring every 15 minutes. Spread on absorbent paper to cool.

116

Small Steps that can make a big fat difference.
(A guide to use to lighten your diet.)

♥ Use Neufchatel for cream cheese, low fat cottage cheese, low fat yogurt, skimmed milk cheeses and 1% milk for any higher fat dairy product.

♥ Cream soups are the most common ingredient in any casserole and the worst nutritionally. They can easily be replaced with chicken stock, wine or a combination, thickened with cornstarch or arrowroot. Add your own fresh mushrooms for an unbeatable cream of mushroom soup base that so many recipes call for. For an even richer base, combine nonfat dry milk with chicken stock and thicken as above.

♥ Cold skimmed evaporated milk with a touch of honey and vanilla is a super whipped topping for desserts. It does take longer to whip but the nutritional gains are worth the extra time. You can also use 2 cups skimmed milk with one teaspoon lemon juice, chill well, then whip. Never use non-dairy whipped toppings. They are chemical non-foods loaded with saturated fat and sugar!

♥ Basting with butter is another frustrating recipe direction for the healthy gourmet. Adapt instead by basting with tomato or lemon juice, stock or wine. Alcohol from the wine evaporates during the cooking process leaving only taste but no calories.

♥ Use only _natural_ peanut butter. Avoid commercial peanut butter at all costs! Commercial peanut butter is not much more than shortening and sugar but fresh ground peanut butter is a great source of healthy protein. If you have trouble switching from the commercial type, begin by mixing it half and half with natural. Gradually increase the proportion of the natural until you have abandoned the commercial type altogether.

♥ Try using legumes (dried beans and peas) as a main dish or a meat substitute for a high nutrition, low fat, low cost meal.

♥ Use safflower, canola oil or olive oil for salads or cooking. They are valuable sources of polyunsaturated and monounsaturated fats.

♥ Purchase tuna packed in water rather than oil to save on unneeded fats.

♥ Non-stick sprays and non-stick skillets are great because they enable you to brown meats without grease.

♥ Dilute soy sauce or tamari sauce half and half with water and 1 teaspoon lemon juice. It increases the flavor and reduces the salt. You may also use low sodium soy sauce.

♥ If not using fresh fruit, use only unsweetened fruits canned or frozen without sugar, packed in their own juices.

♥ Use a little more vanilla and spices in recipes. This will enable you to cut down further on the sugar since vanilla and spices enhance the impression of sweetness and have almost no calories.

♥ Healthy bread crumbs can be made by processing toasted whole wheat bread in a food processor or blender. Unprocessed bran is good too.

♥ Use whole grains anytime a recipe calls for white. Use brown rice instead of white, whole wheat pasta, whole grain crackers in place of saltines, etc.

♥ Substitute fiber and water for laxatives. A laxative isn't the healthy way to get rid of anything; fiber and water are!

♥ Use two egg whites in place of one whole egg. Egg whites are pure protein and egg yolks are pure fat. Also, try this homemade egg substitute: 6 egg whites, 1 Tbsp. safflower oil, 1/4 cup instant non-fat milk powder. Blend till smooth. (1/4 cup = 1 egg)

♥ Recipes calling for sour cream or mayonnaise will usually allow you to substitute plain, low fat yogurt or "blended till smooth" low fat cottage cheese. Great topping for baked potatoes. Add chives or grated parmesan cheese for a low calorie treat.

♥ Try to substitute ground round steak or turkey in place of higher fat meats.

♥ Always remove the skin from chicken <u>before</u>.

For the flavor of butter, but the polyunsaturated to saturated fat ratio and spreadability of corn oil margarine (minus the yellow dyes and preservatives), mix up <u>Better Butter</u>

1 cup safflower oil
1 cup (2 sticks) butter

Blend butter till fluffy, slowly pour in oil until well blended.

If you use margarine, the soft, squeeze kind is best, (less hydrogenation) then tub, then stick. Be sure it's 100% corn oil or safflower oil.

How to add zip to your table decorations

<u>Collections</u> are a wonderful place to start. If you collect antique toys, dolls, paper weights, candlesticks, thimbles, anything; group them together attractively in the center of the table or place a different object at each person's place.

I love beautiful dishes and try to mix in as many odd pieces as possible. Marjolica is marvelous. Depression glass dishes are terrific to collect because they come in so many pretty colors. Pick up unusual dishes at flea markets or tag sales and use them for butter, cookies, relishes, etc. They give your table interest.

I also collect candlesticks and scatter them all around the table. Very romantic.

Hobbies and Special Occasions

If your special guest has a hobby such as tennis, golf, needlework or gourmet cooking, use this as your theme. Fill a cute basket with tennis balls and fill tennis ball cans with ivy and daisies for a centerpiece.

For a golfer - Spray old golf balls a pretty color to match your decor. Fill a basket or glass bowl with them. Circle with ivy, fern or flowers from your yard or the supermarket.

For a needleworker or seamstress, make a floral pin cushion for your centerpiece by bunching small flowers in a bowl. Stick knitting needles among the flowers.

Birthday Party for Guys

Have a football jersey ready to put on the honoree with his age as the numbers on the front and back. Do wonderful things with his hobby or sport. Fill a football helmet with big flowers and put flags in of his favorite teams. You can do almost the same thing with any sport. For example, let your centerpiece be one large flower in a baseball mitt.

If you have a collection of soldiers, trains, any toys for big boys, bring them out now for your centerpiece. Check the kid's toybox.

For a Bridal Luncheon or Shower

Buy several wicker baskets and spray them white. Put a flowering plant in each one. African violets are romantic and inexpensive. Make bows from ribbon that matches your decor. I bought several pairs of porcelain doves on sale and always have them on hand to put beside the baskets. Very romantic. Don't forget the placecards.

Use a basket filled with kitchen utensils for a gift and centerpiece.

A wicker basket for baby.

Bon Voyage Party

Ask your travel agent for posters and flags from different countries. Use big, colorful paper flowers for the centerpiece all bunched in a big basket. Try to find flags of the country they're visiting. If giving a gift, wrap it in a map of the guest of honor's destination.

Decorations

Elaborate or simple, decorations set the mood for an occasion. Use them throughout the whole house when you create your party atmosphere. Use your imagination, personal style and creativity to complement the menu and the style of the occasion.

127

Holidays are a cinch!

Thanksgiving - use a cornucopia filled with gourds, vegetables and fruit. Use a small squash for placecard.

Easter - Use tiny baskets with jelly beans at each place. and an Easter bunny with a basket of eggs for centerpiece.

Valentines - Put red heart shaped doilies on dessert or service plates. Have a heart shaped candy at each plate. Use a white wicker basket filled with a red blooming plant and a bow.

St. Patrick's Day - A shamrock plant is a must. Don't forget Irish stickers on each placecard.

Mother's Day - Gather up old photographs of her and place around the table. Take most any flower. Put a pretty bow for her corsage. She's special.

Father's Day - What's his favorite sport or hobby?   128

Placecards

People love to see their name in print!

Don't consider them pretentious. They are decorative, entertaining and practical. Place-cards can alleviate that uncomfortable silence when your guests arrive at the table. Give them the place they deserve.

Made especially for Sheila

Use a needle with colored thread for the placecard of a needlework lover

Carrie

Use a pin cushion from the dime store with each guest's name.

Use the hundreds of cute stickers now available or glue tiny sea shells, dried flowers, little bow-ties for the men, tiny satin ones for the ladies, on plain cards.

Try never to leave your guests for long periods of time. No party menu should take more than 15 minutes of last minute preparation.

Do not begin to clean up the kitchen while the guests are still present. It makes guests feel obligated to help. They're probably not dressed or in the mood for clean-up duty.

Menu for Dinner for 485

Artichokes Smothered with Herbs
Roast Leg of Lamb with Garlic Guava
Whole Braised Shallots - Carrots Purée
Macédoine of Fruits
Wedding Cake

131

Seated Dinner for 485

Index

Desserts (continued)

Tunnel of Fudge CupCake	88
Tutti Frutti Tortoni	19
Very Easy Ice Cream Pie	71

Fruit

Chutney Peaches	32
Curried Fruit Compote	24
Strawberry Butter	44

Main Dishes

Barbeque Chicken	9
Company Strata	23
Glazed Ham	85
Hopping John	84
Easy Lasagna Bake	17
Mexican Chicken Casserole	62
Oven-smoked Turkey	109
Standing Rib Roast	31
Sunday Best Pot Roast	105

Rules for Perfect

Baked potatoes	102
Crispy Fried Chicken	78
Gelatin Molds	106
Hard Cooked Eggs	77
Iced Tea	11
Meringue	96
Rice	103

Salads

Antipasto	16
Caesar Salad	68
Crab Louis	42
Cranberry Congealed	107
Curried Chicken	41
Guacamole Salad	60
Italian Cole Slaw	86
Polynesian Chicken Salad	40
Classic Potato Salad	80

Sauces and Gravies

Crab Louis Sauce	43
Creamy Bleu Cheese	8
Cream Chicken Gravy	108

Vegetables

Baked Beans the easy way	74
Better-than-Broccoli.	34
Marvelous Rice	33
Peas and Asparagus Casserole	104
Sweet Potato Surprise Balls	110

Some fancy words you need to know.

Bouquet garni- It means a bouquet of herbs tied in cheese-cloth then placed in a simmering sauce, soup or stew.

Au gratin - Any dish topped with breadcrumbs, then browned.

Canapé - A small piece of toasted or fried bread topped with appetizers.

Caviar - The roe or eggs of sturgeon or other large fish, pressed, salted and used as relish.

Welsh rabbit- Melted cheese, usually mixed with milk, or beer and served over toast or crackers.

Look for These Other Books by Carolyn Coats and Pamela Smith

Things Your Mother Always Told You But You Didn't Want to Hear
Warm, witty, nostalgic words of wisdom you'll remember forever with love.
ISBN 0-7852-8056-1

Things Your Dad Always Told You But You Didn't Want to Hear
Funny, profound, memorable. The perfect companion to the "Mother" book. Great for men's and boys' birthday gifts.
ISBN 0-7852-8055-3

My Grandmother Always Said That
From generation to generation, grandmothers have always said the same wise words to their families. They do it because they love them, but mostly because they just can't help it.
ISBN 0-7852-8053-7

Me, A Gourmet Cook?
A delightful cookbook full of easy but delicious recipes and creative, entertaining ideas. Perfect for graduation and new brides and grooms.
ISBN 0-7852-8052-9

Alive and Well in the Fast Lane
The very latest information on how to lower your cholesterol and risk of cancer; how to increase your energy and stamina and achieve your ideal weight. The 10 Commandments of good nutrition plus great recipes and tips.
ISBN 0-7852-8050-2

Perfectly Pregnant!
The latest information to perfectly nourish you and your baby —hints to overcome morning sickness, assure ideal weight gain, and maintain your energy and stamina. The perfect gift for that "special lady."
ISBN 0-7852-8054-5

Come Cook With Me!
Shhh . . . Don't tell the kids, but this wonderful book has recipes that are delicious, fun to make AND nutritious. The gift every grandmother and parent will love to give.
ISBN 0-7852-8051-0

Available at fine bookstores everywhere.
THOMAS NELSON PUBLISHERS
Nashville, Tennessee 37214

Published in Nashville, Tennessee, by Thomas Nelson, Inc., Publishers, and distributed in Canada by Word Communications, Ltd., Richmond, British Columbia, and in the United Kingdom by Word (UK), Ltd., Milton Keynes, England.

Library of Congress information

Coats, Carolyn, 1935-
    Me, a gourmet cook? / written by Carolyn Coats ; illustrations by Sheila Behr.
      p.   cm.
    Originally published: Orlando, Fla. : Carolyn Coats' Bestsellers, c1985.
    Includes index.
    ISBN: 0-7852-8052-9 (pbk.)
    1. Entertaining. 2. Cookery. 3. Menus. I. Title.
TX731.C6 1994
642'.4—dc20

93-42304
CIP

Printed in the United States of America

1 2 3 4 5 6 7 - 99 98 97 96 95 94